SOUTH SAN FRANCISCO LIBRARY
3 9048 00024446 4
W9-BSW-602
SSF

# VOLCANOES

Lily Wood

PHOTO CREDITS: Cover: SuperStock. 1: Bernhard Edmaier/Photo Researchers; 3: AP/Wide World Photos; 4: Hawaiian Volcano Observatory/United States Geological Survey; 5: National Oceanographic and Atmospheric Administration; 7: Tom & Pat Leeson/Photo Researchers; 8: Frans Lanting/Tony Stone Images; 9: USGS; 10: Mark Newman/Photo Researchers; 11: Francois Gohier/Photo Researchers; 12-13: R.G.K. Photography/Tony Stone Images; 14: Brian Miller/Bruce Coleman Inc.; 15: Charlie Ott/Photo Researchers; 16: Adam G. Sylvester/Photo Researchers; 17: Kevin West, AP/Wide World Photos; 18: David Frazier/Photo Researchers; 19: David Frazier/Photo Researchers; 20-21: SuperStock; 22: SuperStock; 24: David Hardy/Photo Researchers; 25: R.P. Hoblitt/USGS; 27: Bernhard Edmaier/ Photo Researchers; 28: University of Colorado/NOAA; 30: Russell D. Curtis/Photo Researchers; 31: Russell D. Curtis/Photo Researchers; 32: G. Brad Lewis/Tony Stone Images; 34: SuperStock; 35: John McConnico, AP/Wide World Photos; 37: SuperStock; 39: Matthew Shipp/Photo Researchers; 40: Zoltan Gaal Jr./Photo Researchers; 41: John Marshall/Tony Stone Images; 43: Piero Pomponi/Liaison Agency; 44: Krafft/Photo Researchers.



Library of Congress Cataloging-in-Publication Data available.

ISBN 0-439-29585-8

*Book design by Barbara Balch and Kay Petronio*
*Photo research by Sarah Longacre*

10 9 8 7 6 5 4 3 2 1    01 02 03 04

Printed in the U.S.A. 23

First trade printing, August 2001

We are grateful to Francie Alexander, reading specialist, and to Adele M. Brodkin, Ph.D., developmental psychologist, for their contributions to the development of this series.

Our thanks also to our science consultant Christina Heliker at the United States Geological Survey Hawaiian Volcano Observatory.

*Kaboom! Whoosh! Ssssss!*

**Volcanoes** can be loud and exciting. When they blow their tops, rocks shoot through the air. Ash clouds rise. Melted rock flows like rivers. It glows red. It sizzles. It could even melt a car!

Volcanoes are vents, or openings, in the Earth. They let heat from deep inside the Earth escape. Vents in the top of a baking pie do the same thing. Steam rises and hot juice bubbles out of slits cut in a pie. But don't expect cherry filling from volcanoes! Volcanoes spout steam, **ash**, gases, and melted rock. This activity is called an **eruption** (ee-**ruhp**-shuhn).

In 1980, the ground shook in Washington State. Mount St. Helens rumbled. Then...*bang!* It erupted. The side of the volcano exploded. The top of the mountain was suddenly gone. A cloud of steam and ash rose. Rocks, ash, and hot gases rushed down the volcano. The blast knocked over trees as far as 6 miles (10 kilometers) away!

As the eruption continued, mudslides started. The volcano's heat melted snow and ice, creating meltwater. This water mixed with ash and dirt, making mud. The mud poured down the mountain. It buried houses, trucks, and streets. Most people escaped. But sixty-two people were killed by the eruption. Almost all the plants and animals in a 150-square-mile (388-square-kilometer) area died. A few insects, spiders, frogs, toads, and gophers survived because they were in burrows underground.

*This house was destroyed by the mud flow from Mount St. Helens. The residents had already fled.*

Eruptions, like Mount St. Helens, start out deep in the Earth. Earth has three layers: the crust, the mantle, and the core. We live on the top layer, the crust. Animals, plants, and soil are also atop the crust.

*Golden lava, Pu`u `O`o Volcano, Hawaii*

Deep down, 3 to 25 miles (5 to 40 kilometers) below the crust, is a soft, hot layer. This is the mantle.The mantle contains hot, melted rock called **magma**. Magma rises from the mantle. In certain places, it pushes through the crust. This creates volcanoes. When magma comes out of a volcano, it is called **lava**.

*Lava fountain, Pu`u `O`o Volcano, Hawaii*

A volcanic eruption can last hours, days, weeks, or years. Each volcano erupts in a different way. Hawaiian volcanoes erupt fairly quietly, without big explosions. Lava spills out of the volcanoes. Or it sprays out, like a fountain.

Visitors can safely watch eruptions in Hawaii Volcanoes National Park. Rangers keep people from getting too close to the hot lava. Lava can be 2100°F (1148°C). That is hot enough to melt some metals.

The lava flows out at speeds of 6 miles (10 kilometers) per hour. So scientists keep watch over volcanoes and flowing lava. In Hawaii, rangers close roads when lava is flowing nearby. They make sure there is time to get out of the way of the lava. But later the lava may cover roads and houses. When the lava cools, it forms rock.

*The owners were gone by the time lava flow from a volcano set this house aflame.*

pahoehoe

In Hawaii, you can see two kinds of lava. Some lava hardens into shiny, rounded, wrinkled *pahoehoe* (pa-**hoh**-ee-**hoh**-ee). Stickier lava cools to form rough, sharp-edged *`a`a.*

People say that Hawaiians named this lava *`a`a* because walking barefoot on the sharp pieces makes them shout “Ah, ah!”

Lava forms several different kinds of rocks. You may find tuff, obsidian, or pumice in your local rock shop or museum.

Tuff is made from layers of ash that harden.

## Take a Closer Look

*Close-up of obsidian*

Glassy obsidian is made from quickly cooling lava. Ancient peoples used it to make tools such as arrowheads.

Pumice shoots out of volcanoes. Gas bubbles escaping from cooling lava make holes in this airy kind of rock. Pumice is so light, it floats on water.

Volcanoes are studied by scientists called **volcanologists** (vol-kuhn-**ol**-uh-jists). Volcanologists often walk on erupting volcanoes. Their work can be dangerous and flowing lava is not the only danger.

*A pyroclastic flow surges down the side of a volcano toward a residential area.*

**Pyroclastic** (pye-roh-**klass**-tik) **flows** are boiling hot rivers of gas, ash, and pumice. They flow down volcanoes. They move at speeds of 150 miles (241 kilometers) per hour or more.

*Mount St. Helens cleanup*

Ash also shoots up into the sky, making a huge, dark cloud. Then it spreads and falls like snow. Ash can fill the sky, making noon look like night. Ash may pile up on roofs and streets in thick layers. The weight of the ash can make roofs fall in.

*Protection from Mount St. Helens ash*

After some eruptions, there is so much ash in the air that it can clog a person's nose and mouth. The ash makes it hard to breathe. Breathing large amounts of ash can cause lung disease.

*Tourists visit the ruins of the Forum in Pompeii. Mount Vesuvius is in the background.*

Today, scientists can usually warn people when a volcanic eruption is coming. But 2000 years ago, volcanic ash buried a town without warning. In 79 A.D., the volcano Vesuvius erupted in Italy.

Rock, ash, gases, and mud covered the towns of Pompeii and Herculaneum. About 3,360 people died. The ash and mud covered their bodies. Later, it hardened around them.

Over the years, many of the bodies decayed. But the empty spaces, shaped like the bodies, remained. In the 1800s, scientists called archaeologists (ahr-kee-**ol**-uh-jists) poured plaster into these holes. The plaster took the shape of the bodies. Archaeologists have learned about ancient life from studying these plaster models.

In May of 1883, the island of Krakatau blew up. This Indonesian island was the top of an erupting volcano. The sound of the explosion was one of the loudest noises ever heard. Dust and ash from the eruption traveled around the Earth.

## Take a Look Back

*Artwork showing the eruption of Krakatau*

*House covered with ash, Mount Pinatubo, Philippines*

In 1991, Mount Pinatubo in the Philippines erupted, making lots of ash. Many people in the Philippines wore masks to keep ash out of their lungs. Both Krakatau and Mount Pinatubo are still erupting. But recent eruptions have not been as strong.

"Active" volcanoes are erupting or have erupted in the last 10,000 years. Earth has more than 1,500 active volcanoes. Most are under the ocean. Some are on land. About 60 volcanoes erupt each year.

Canada has about 20 volcanoes. The United States and its territories have more than 100. Mexico's 35 volcanoes include Popocatépetl, Colima, and El Chichón. The world's largest volcano is Mauna Loa in Hawaii. One of the world's most active volcanoes is Kilauea, also in Hawaii.

Central America, South America, and Asia have lots of volcanoes. The Arenal volcano is in Costa Rica. The Tambora volcano is in Indonesia.

*Lava flowing from Mount Etna glows in the night.*

Europe and Africa have volcanoes, too. Italy's Mount Etna is a volcano on the island of Sicily. Mount Etna is one of Europe's most active volcanoes.

Even Antarctica has volcanoes. But Australia has no active ones.

On Earth, most volcanoes lie on borders between tectonic (tek-**tah**-nik) plates. These plates are pieces of Earth's crust. They float, like rafts, on the mantle. Where the plates rub together, volcanoes form. Volcanoes also form where plates pull apart.

Many volcanoes are located on the edge of the Pacific Plate. These volcanoes are called the **Ring of Fire**. Japan, Alaska, Washington, Oregon, California, Chile, and New Zealand are all in the Ring of Fire. There are more than 70 active volcanoes in Japan alone!

*Mount Ngauruhoe, New Zealand*

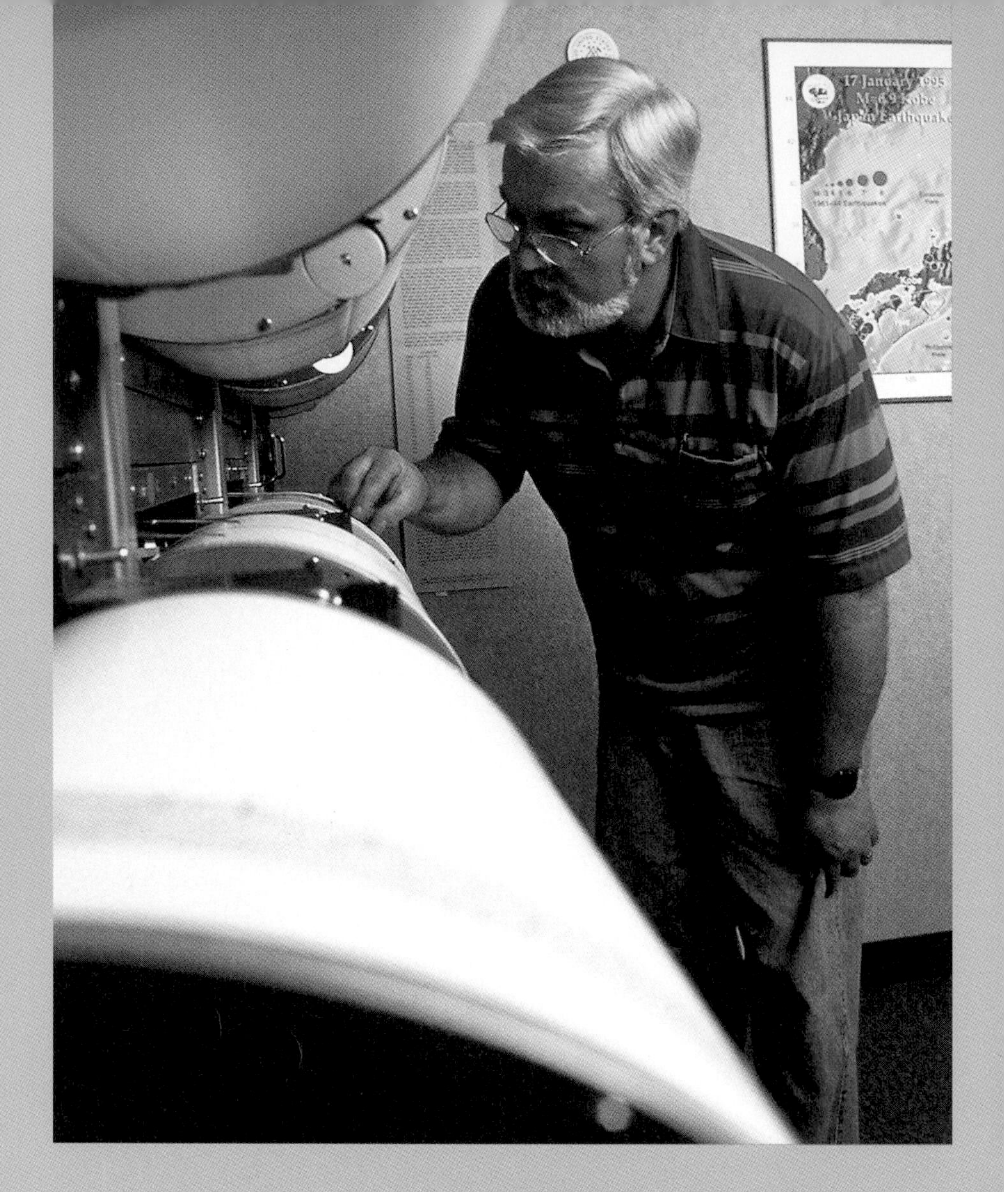


Like volcanoes, earthquakes are common at plate edges. When tectonic plates shift, the Earth shakes.

Magma, moving inside a volcano, can cause earthquakes, too.

Earthquakes and eruptions often go together. Volcanologists measure earthquakes using a seismometer (size-**mah**-muh-tur). Earthquakes can be a sign that a volcano will erupt soon.

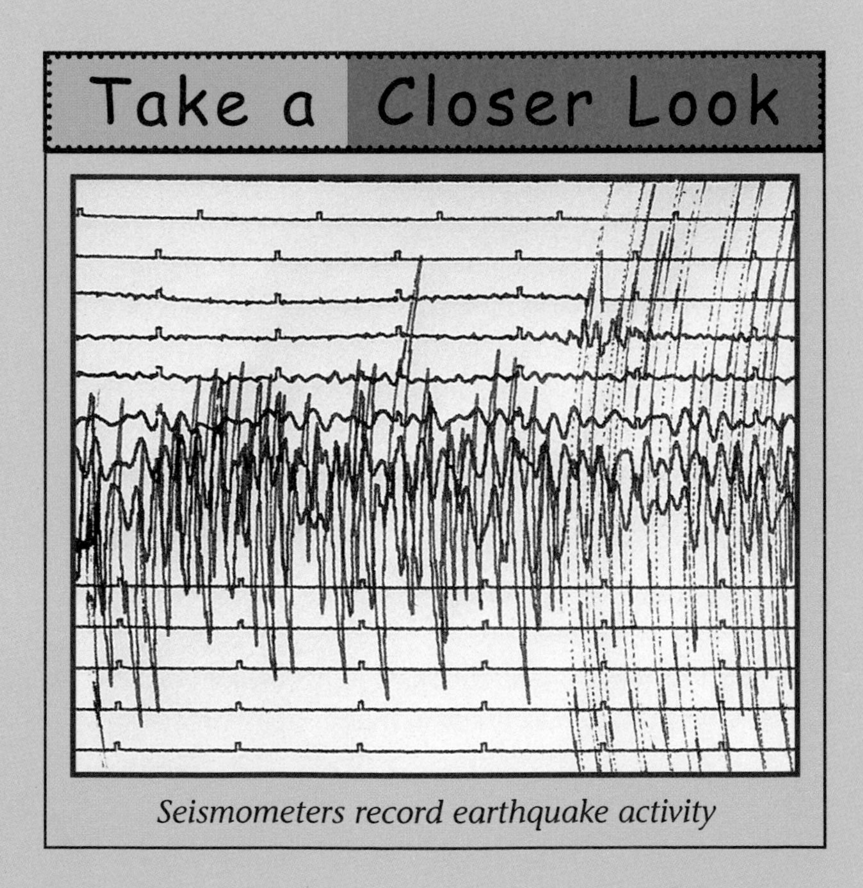


*Seismometers record earthquake activity*

Some volcanoes are not between plates. They form over "hot spots" in the mantle. The active Hawaiian volcanoes are over a hot spot.

Volcanic eruptions are hard to predict. A volcano can suddenly stop erupting. It may erupt again the next day, or not for thousands of years.

*Lava flow, Hawaii*

*Montserrat before the eruption*

For almost 400 years, the Soufrière Hills volcano on the Caribbean island of Montserrat was quiet. Then, in 1992, the island started having a lot of earthquakes. Volcanologists said an eruption was coming.

On July 18, 1995, the volcano began erupting. Ash, hot gases, and lava came out of the volcano. Lava and ash buried much of the island. People had to leave their homes. But they had plenty of warning, because of volcanologists' predictions.

*A church in Montserrat lies beneath up to 10 feet (3 meters) of ash after the eruption.*

Over time, volcanoes usually grow bigger. Magma inside the volcano pushes upward. This makes the volcano taller. Lava flows out, cools, and hardens. It forms rock. Layers of ash harden. The land builds up, layer by layer.

In this way, undersea volcanoes grow tall. When their tops poke up above the waves, islands are born. In 1963, a volcano near Iceland erupted. Lava from the volcano flowed out. It built a new island called Surtsey.

Hawaiian islands form the same way. In Hawaii, lava pours into the ocean. It cools, creating new land. It adds new area to the islands each year.

*Surtsey Volcano, Iceland*

Volcanoes can sometimes be helpful. Ash from volcanoes makes soil good for plants. Rocks from volcanoes are used to build houses. Crushed volcanic rock is used in soaps, cleansers, concrete, and plaster.

Heat from volcanoes helps warm swimming pools and houses in Iceland. Heat from volcanoes is also used to make electricity.

*Krafla Volcano, Iceland*

After an eruption, the area around a volcano looks dead. Mud, lava, and ash cover the land.

*Mount St. Helens area right after the eruption*

But soon the wind carries seeds onto the cooled lava. The seeds sprout and grow. Forests can grow. Animals move back onto the land.

*Green, growing flowers and plants returned to Mount St. Helens slowly in the months after the eruption.*

Many people live near volcanoes. They have to be ready for eruptions. Some cities have evacuation plans, in case the people need to move to a safer area.

In the South American country of Ecuador, some people hold volcano drills, just like we hold fire drills.

A siren sounds. Children and adults climb the highest hill in town. There they hope to be safe from mudslides.

*The city of Quito, Ecuador, is in the foothills of the Guagua Pichincha Volcano.*

Today, volcanologists are trying to improve their predictions. Better predictions would give people more time to leave the area before an eruption. And people would know not to go into a dangerous area. Recently, a scientist began studying volcano sounds. He uses special microphones to listen to the magma moving inside a volcano. His work may make predictions more accurate.

Volcanologists still have a lot to learn. They always have more questions than answers. But that is part of what makes their work so exciting!

# Glossary

**ash**—tiny particles of rock that come out of a volcano

**eruption** (ee-**ruhp**-shuhn)—what happens when a volcano spurts out gas, lava, ash, and/or pumice

**lava**—liquid rock at the Earth's surface, or lava that has cooled to form rock

**magma**—melted rock that is underground

**pyroclastic** (pye-roh-**klass**-tik) **flows**—rivers of hot gases, ash, and pumice that erupt from volcanoes and flow down their sides

**Ring of Fire**—the volcanoes that border the Pacific Plate and Pacific Ocean

**volcanoes**—vents in the surface of Earth that erupt lava, ash, or gases

**volcanologists** (vol-kuhn-**ol**-uh-jists)—scientists who study volcanoes

# Index

# A Note to Parents

Learning to read is such an exciting time in a child's life. You may delight in sharing your favorite fairy tales and picture books with your child.

But don't forget the importance of introducing your child to the world of nonfiction. The ability to read and comprehend factual material will be essential to your child in school, and throughout life. The Scholastic Science Readers™ series was created especially with beginning readers in mind. These books, with their clear texts and beautiful photographs, will help you to share the wonders of science with *your* new reader.

# Suggested Activity

Readers in Oregon, Hawaii, Alaska, Washington, Wyoming, Montana, and Idaho are fortunate to live in states that have national parks which focus on volcanoes and volcanism. If you don't live in these areas, think creatively! A visit to your local natural history museum or rock shop is likely to turn up samples of volcanic rock of some sort. Look for pumice, tuff, or obsidian. Even the local beauty supply store can be a source of pumice. Simply holding a pumice stone in his or her hand can give your child a true-to-life connection to faraway volcanoes!